BOND
COCKTAILS

BOND
COCKTAILS

OVER 20 CLASSIC COCKTAIL RECIPES
FOR THE SECRET AGENT IN ALL OF US

KATHERINE BEBO

RYLAND PETERS & SMALL
LONDON • NEW YORK

For Ben, the Man with the Golden Pun. You leave me shaken, stirred and everything in-between!

Designer Geoff Borin
Commissioning Editor Nathan Joyce
Production Controller Mai-Ling Collyer
Art Director Leslie Harrington
Editorial Director Julia Charles
Publisher Cindy Richards

Indexer Vanessa Bird

First published in 2015 by
Ryland Peters & Small
20–21 Jockey's Fields
London WC1R 4BW
and
341 East 116th Street
New York, 10029

www.rylandpeters.com

10 9 8 7 6 5 4 3

Recipes on pages 13, 14, 17, 18, 21, 25, 28, 32, 41, 45, 46, 55, 56, 59, 60 and 63 © Ben Reed 2015. Recipes on pages 31, 35, 36, 42, 48 and 50 © Tristan Stephenson. All other text © Ryland Peters & Small 2015.

Design and photographs © Ryland Peters & Small 2015.
For other picture credits, please see page 64.

ISBN: 978-1-78879-144-1

A CIP record for this book is available from the British Library.

US Library of Congress CIP data has been applied for.

Printed in China

NOTES

• When using slices of citrus fruits, try to find organic, unwaxed fruits and wash well before using. If you can only find treated fruit, scrub well in warm soapy water and rinse well before using.

• Measurements are occasionally given in barspoons, which are equivalent to 5 ml or 1 teaspoon.

CONTENTS

LIVE & LET DRINK

Aside from the beautiful women, fast cars, crazy gadgets, death-defying stunts, achingly suave tuxedos and double entendres à go-go, James Bond is also known for being partial to a tipple or two. In the *You Only Live Twice* novel alone, he knocked back over 225 units of alcohol. That's equivalent to approximately 113 vodka martinis (shaken, not stirred, naturally). But it's not always Bond's signature vodtini (first appearing in the book *Dr. No* – once with a twist of lime and once with a twist of lemon) that crosses his lips. In fact, throughout the books, he only drinks 35 martinis compared to over 100 whisky-based drinks.

POURS GALORE

Yes, the debonair spy consumes many a diverse beverage – from a Mint Julep to a Mojito, from a Sazerac to a Stinger. He devours 317 alcoholic drinks throughout the novels: that's one drink every seven pages. It's a wonder he's able to fire his gun straight. It seems that while the silver-tongued secret agent has a licence to kill, he also holds a licence to spill.

THE MAN WITH THE GOLDEN GIN

Moving to the silver screen, whether it's Sean Connery having a bath next to bottles of vodka and vermouth (you never know when the urge for a cocktail might strike) in *Diamonds Are Forever*; Timothy Dalton quaffing a flute of Bollinger champagne in *The Living Daylights*, or Daniel Craig elaborately ordering a Vesper cocktail in *Casino Royale*, alcohol plays as important a role in the series as the villains, Bond girls and unfeasible escape routes.

DRINK ANOTHER DAY

Bond himself acknowledges that he's fond of a beverage. In *Thunderball*, he comments: 'It's just that I'd rather die of drink than of thirst.' Even the day after a heavy night, he opts for 'hair of the dog' as a hangover cure: 'Brandy with club soda and a couple of Phensic tablets'. Daniel Craig, Bond #6, concurs: 'Bond is a drinker, he always has been.'

So, embrace the sharp shooter's love of shots with this collection of enticing cocktails, each as cool, smooth and refined as the man himself: Bond, James Bond.

Q BRANCH

Where would James Bond be without the trusty Q? Using lame walkie-talkies and cheap digital watches, most likely. A bartender without the right tools is like an international spy without the right gadgets. Stock up on these cocktail essentials so that you can mix things up, espionage style.

MEASURE/JIGGER
Bond is extremely measured. You should be too with a measure/jigger. The dual measure is a good choice as it holds both 50 ml/1⅔ fl. oz and 25 ml/¾ fl. oz. (a double and a single shot).

SHAKER
How can you possibly make a martini, shaken not stirred, without a shaker? Opt for either the stylish Boston shaker, which is half stainless steel, half glass, or the more traditional shaker with the inbuilt strainer and twist-off cap.

BAR SPOON
The bar spoon – with its long, spiralling handle – is useful for stirring drinks and the gentle pouring needed for layered cocktails. The flat end can be used to crush ingredients too.

MUDDLER
There's no need to go all 'Xenia Onatopp' – the femme fatale in the film *GoldenEye* who crushes her unfortunate victims to death with her rather well-toned thighs – when using a muddler. Simply use this wooden pestle to crush sugar cubes, lemons, limes and herbs.

GLASSES

THE MARTINI GLASS
A martini glass acts like an extension to Bond's hand for much of the time. With its open face and slim stem, it epitomizes the cool elegance vital for his signature drink.

THE COCKTAIL GLASS
The cocktail glass is similar to the martini glass but with a slightly rounded bowl.

rocks, it sits comfortably in the hand and, like the Ice Palace in *Die Another Day*, will leave you feeling suitably chilled.

THE SHOT GLASS
Take your best shot with this small, but reliably sturdy glass. Aim... fire!

THE CHAMPAGNE FLUTE
With its long stem and narrow rim, this elegant glass is perfect for keeping the sparkle in your bubbly.

THE HIGHBALL AND THE COLLINS GLASS
Reminiscent of the Bond girls, Highball and Collins glasses come in various sizes and are tall, slim and elegant, designed to keep a long drink fresh.

THE ROCKS OR OLD FASHIONED GLASS
This is a squat, straight-sided glass on a heavy base. Perfect for a drink on the

THE CHAMPAGNE COUPE
A shallow, broad-bowled glass, often stacked to build towers of free-flowing Champagne.

MIXING GLASS
This is used with a strainer for making drinks that are... wait for it... stirred, not shaken. Gasp!

FROM RUSSIA WITH LOVE

BOND'S COCKTAIL OF CHOICE IS THE VODKA MARTINI. IT MUST, OF COURSE, BE SHAKEN, NOT STIRRED – A CATCHPHRASE THAT'S TAKEN ON A LIFE OF ITS OWN. THROUGHOUT IAN FLEMING'S NOVELS AND SHORT STORIES, THE SECRET SERVICE AGENT ORDERS OVER 20 VODKA MARTINIS. GET SHAKING WITH THESE VODKA COCKTAILS WITH A TWIST.

1

CLASSIC MARTINI

AS SYNONYMOUS WITH THE JAMES BOND
FRANCHISE AS INNUENDOS, LUDICROUS
STUNTS AND ALWAYS GETTING THE GIRL,
THE MARTINI WILL FOREVER BE ASSOCIATED
WITH 007.

a dash of vermouth
(Noilly Prat or Martini
Extra Dry)

**75 ml/2½ fl. oz. well-
chilled gin or vodka**

**an olive or lemon twist,
to garnish**

Add the vermouth and the gin
or vodka to a mixing glass filled
with ice and stir. Strain into a
chilled martini glass and garnish
with an olive or lemon twist.

VODKA MARTINI

IN MOST FILMS, THE REQUEST FOR A VODKA MARTINI IS FOLLOWED WITH 'SHAKEN, NOT STIRRED'. HOWEVER, IN *CASINO ROYALE*, WHEN THE EVER-COOL DANIEL CRAIG IS ASKED, 'SHAKEN OR STIRRED?' HE REPLIES, 'DO I LOOK LIKE I GIVE A DAMN?'

a dash of dry vermouth

50 ml/1²/₃ fl. oz. vodka

a pitted olive or lemon zest, to garnish

Fill a mixing glass with ice and stir with a barspoon until the glass is chilled. Tip the water out and top with ice. Add the vermouth and continue stirring. Strain the liquid away and top with ice. Add the vodka and stir in a continuous circular motion until the vodka is thoroughly chilled (taking care not to chip the ice). Strain into a frosted martini glass and garnish with either a pitted olive or lemon zest.

VESPER

'THREE MEASURES OF GORDON'S, ONE OF VODKA, HALF A MEASURE OF KINA LILLET. SHAKE IT VERY WELL UNTIL IT'S ICE-COLD, THEN ADD A LARGE THIN SLICE OF LEMON PEEL. GOT IT? THIS DRINK'S MY OWN INVENTION. I'M GOING TO PATENT IT WHEN I THINK OF A GOOD NAME' – *CASINO ROYALE* (NOVEL). WHEN BOND MEETS SEXY VESPER LYND, BOY, DOES HE THINK OF A GOOD NAME!

60 ml/2 fl. oz. gin

20 ml/²⁄₃ fl. oz. vodka

10 ml/¹⁄₃ fl. oz. Kina Lillet
(French vermouth)

**a long lemon peel,
to garnish**

Add all the ingredients to a shaker filled with ice, shake and strain into a frosted martini glass. Garnish with the lemon peel and serve.

DIRTY MARTINI

IN *SPECTRE*, BOND SHAKES THINGS UP BY DRINKING A DIRTY MARTINI, RATHER THAN HIS CLASSIC VODKA MARTINI. WHY? SOME SAY HE WAS TRYING TO IMPRESS HIS SEXY FRENCH DINING COMPANION, DR MADELEINE SWANN. IT WORKS – SHE PASSIONATELY ACCEPTS HIS OLIVE BRANCH.

a dash of vermouth
(Noilly Prat or Martini Extra Dry)

75 ml/2½ fl. oz. freezing gin or vodka

a large dash of brine from the olive or onion jar

an olive, a lemon twist or a cocktail onion, to garnish

Add all the ingredients to a shaker filled with ice, shake sharply, and strain into a frosted martini glass. Garnish with an olive, a lemon twist or a cocktail onion.

SMOKY MARTINI

IN THE NOVELS, BOND PUFFED OVER 70
CIGARETTES A DAY. WHEN ROGER MOORE –
AN AVID CIGAR SMOKER – WAS CAST AS BOND,
HE DECIDED HE WANTED TO SMOKE CIGARS
INSTEAD, SO HAD IT WRITTEN INTO HIS
CONTRACT THAT THERE WOULD BE AN
UNLIMITED SUPPLY OF CIGARS ON SET.

75 ml/2½ fl. oz. gin

a dash of dry vermouth

a dash of whisky

an olive or a lemon twist, to garnish

Add the gin, a dash of dry vermouth and a dash of whisky to a shaker filled with cracked ice. Shake sharply and strain into a frosted martini glass with a lemon-zested rim. Garnish with an olive or a lemon twist.

NAKED *OR* CHURCHILL MARTINI

IF THERE'S ONE THING JAMES BOND IS GOOD AT, IT'S MAKING WOMEN LOSE THEIR CLOTHES. WITH SEX SCENES UNDER A PARACHUTE, WHILE SCUBA DIVING, IN A STEAM ROOM, IN OUTER SPACE... THIS SPY SURE LIKES TO LOVE ON THE WILD SIDE.

50 ml/1²/₃ fl. oz. gin

1 bottle dry vermouth

pitted green olives, to garnish

Using a mixing glass, chill a large shot of gin over ice and pour into a frosted martini glass. And the dry vermouth? Well, it doesn't actually feature. The reason why it's also called the Churchill Martini is because the great man was tired of his beloved martini being sabotaged by too much vermouth, so, he'd just look at the vermouth bottle when fixing himself a martini!

BLOOD MARTINI

THERE'S NO DENYING THE BOND MOVIES ARE VIOLENT: THE BODY COUNT FROM THE OFFICIAL FILMS ALONE IS OVER 1,300. *YOU ONLY LIVE TWICE* WAS THE MOST DEADLY FILM WITH 196 DEMISES. PIERCE BROSNAN WAS THE MOST LETHAL BOND, WITH 135 KILLS UNDER HIS PRADA BELT. BANG!

50 ml/1²/₃ fl. oz. vodka

15 ml/¹/₂ fl. oz. Campari

10 ml/¹/₃ fl. oz. framboise

5 ml/1 teaspoon fresh lime juice

30 ml/1 fl. oz. cranberry juice

a dash of Cointreau

orange zest, to garnish

Add all the ingredients to a shaker filled with ice, shake sharply and strain into a frosted martini glass. Garnish with orange zest.

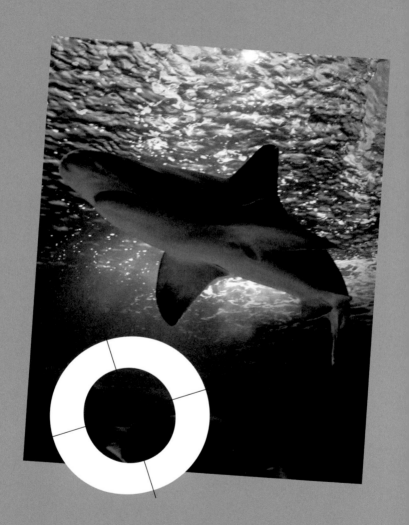

JAWS: BEVERAGES WITH BITE

ONE OF THE MOST MEMORABLE HENCHMEN IN THE BOND SERIES, JAWS IS ONLY TOO HAPPY TO PROVIDE A SERIOUS BITE – AS DO THESE COCKTAILS. JAWS IS MUTE IN BOTH *THE SPY WHO LOVED ME* AND *MOONRAKER*, EXCEPT FOR HIS ONE LINE: 'WELL, HERE'S TO US!' AFTER POPPING A BOTTLE OF CHAMPAGNE WITH HIS TEETH TO SHARE WITH HIS NEW GIRLFRIEND.

SAZERAC

TRANSPORT YOURSELF TO NEW ORLEANS IN *LIVE AND LET DIE* AND SIP A SAZERAC ALONG WITH BOND AND CIA AGENT FELIX LEITER. THEN, AS THE KICK OF THE ABSINTHE HITS YOUR THROAT, IMAGINE JAWS BITING THROUGH THE THICK CABLE CAR WIRE IN *MOONRAKER*, WHICH WAS ACTUALLY MADE OF LIQUORICE.

50 ml/1²/₃ fl. oz. rye whiskey

10 ml/2 barspoons sugar syrup (2:1 ratio of sugar to water, heated until the sugar dissolves)

2 dashes Peychaud's bitters

10 ml/2 barspoons absinthe

a thin lemon zest, to garnish

Stir all the ingredients, except the absinthe, in a mixing glass filled with ice. Rinse a chilled rocks glass with the absinthe. Strain the contents of the mixing glass into the rocks glass, and garnish with lemon zest.

NEGRONI

IN *THUNDERBALL*, AFTER BOND HAS DISARMED
A GOON WITH A GUN, HE REWARDS HIMSELF
WITH A NEGRONI. HE ALSO ORDERS HIMSELF
THIS DRINK IN IAN FLEMING'S SHORT STORY
RISICO.

**25 ml/¾ fl. oz. Tanqueray
No. Ten gin**

25 ml/¾ fl. oz. Campari

**25 ml/¾ fl. oz. Martini
Rosso vermouth**

**a slice of lemon (or
grapefruit), to garnish**

Stir all the ingredients over
cubed ice for 60 seconds, then
strain into a chilled rocks glass
with cubed ice (or use a large
hand-cracked piece of ice).
Garnish with the lemon (or
grapefruit).

STINGER

NOT SEEN IN ANY OF THE MOVIES – PERHAPS BECAUSE IT LACKS THE MACHO FACTOR – THE STINGER IS A FAVOURITE IN THE *DIAMONDS ARE FOREVER* NOVEL. ALSO, IT IS PAIRED WITH COFFEE IN *THUNDERBALL* AT THE CASINO BAR BEFORE BOND AND FELIX HIT THE TABLES.

50 ml/1²⁄₃ fl. oz. brandy

25 ml/³⁄₄ fl. oz. crème de menthe (white)

Add the ingredients to a shaker filled with ice, shake and strain into a frosted martini glass.

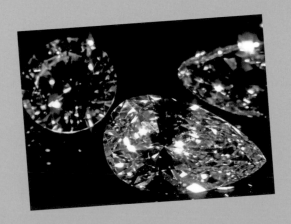

SIDECAR

MIX YOURSELF A SIDECAR AS YOU WATCH BOND AND AGENT TRIPLE X ESCAPE DEATH FROM A MOTORBIKE-SIDECAR BOMB ON THE LOOSE IN *THE SPY WHO LOVED ME*. IT'LL BE NOTHING SHORT OF EXPLOSIVE!

40 ml/1⅓ fl. oz. Hennessy Fine de Cognac

20 ml/⅔ fl. oz. Cointreau

20 ml/⅔ fl. oz. freshly squeezed lemon juice

Shake all the ingredients together with cubed ice, then fine strain into a chilled Champagne coupe glass. That's it!

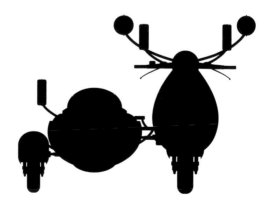

CORPSE REVIVER

CONCOCT THIS DRINK FOR *SKYFALL*, IN WHICH BOND IS SHOT AND 'KILLED'. THEN POUR YOURSELF ANOTHER TO GET OVER THE SHOCK, BEFORE REJOICING WITH YET ANOTHER WHEN HE 'COMES BACK FROM THE DEAD'.

30 ml/1 fl. oz. Hennessy Fine de Cognac

30 ml/1 fl. oz. Calvados

30 ml/1 fl. oz. Martini Rosso vermouth

Stir all the ingredients together with cubed ice and strain into a chilled champagne coupe glass.

SKYFALL HIGHBALLS

IN *SKYFALL*, THERE WAS MUCH DISCUSSION ABOUT THE FACT THAT, IN THE NAME OF PRODUCT PLACEMENT, BOND CRACKED OPEN A...GASP...HEINEKEN BEER! BUT, FEAR NOT, THERE'S ALSO A SUITABLE AMOUNT OF HARD LIQUOR IN THE FILM, WHICH INSPIRED THESE SMOOTH, LONG COCKTAILS.

MOSCOW MULE

RUSSIA'S CAPITAL CITY, MOSCOW, FEATURES IN THE NOVELS *THE MAN WITH THE GOLDEN GUN* AND *THE MAN FROM BARBAROSSA*. AND THE FILMS AREN'T SHORT OF RUSSIAN CHARACTERS – FROM BADDIES TO BOND GIRLS, FROM KGB MAJORS TO, ER, ROBBIE COLTRANE.

50 ml/1²/₃ fl. oz. vodka

¹/₂ lime

ginger beer, to top up

Pour the vodka into a highball glass filled with ice. Squeeze the lime, cut into four, into the glass. Top with ginger beer and stir with a barspoon. Serve with a straw.

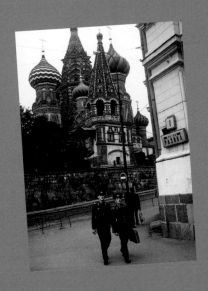

MOJITO

IN *DIE ANOTHER DAY*, BOND OFFERS JINX A TASTE OF HIS MOJITO AFTER SHE SEDUCTIVELY SASHAYS OUT OF THE SURF IN HER ORANGE BIKINI. IT'S A WONDERFUL PREAMBLE TO THE ONSLAUGHT OF SEXUAL INNUENDOS THAT FOLLOW.

10 fresh mint leaves, plus a large mint sprig, to garnish

50 ml/1²/₃ fl. oz. Bacardi Superior rum

25 ml/³/₄ fl. oz. freshly squeezed lime juice

12.5 ml/¹/₂ fl. oz. sugar syrup (2:1 ratio of sugar to water, heated in a saucepan until the sugar dissolves)

soda water, to top up

Gently muddle (see page 8) the mint, to release its oils and flavours, in the base of a chilled highball glass. Be careful not to crush the mint, though. Add the rum, lime juice and sugar syrup. Stir gently and add a little crushed ice. Stir some more and continue adding ice until the glass is full. Give everything a good churn and add a splash of soda. Cap off with more crushed ice and add a sprig of mint on top. (Give the mint sprig a slap on a firm surface just before serving to release some of the aroma into the air.)

MINT JULEP

ARCH-ENEMY AURIC GOLDFINGER PROFFERS BOND A MINT JULEP WHILE AT HIS KENTUCKY HORSE RANCH, ASSURING HIM THAT THE DRINK IS 'TRADITIONAL, BUT SATISFYING'. BOND RESPONDS WITH: 'SOUR MASH, BUT NOT TOO SWEET, PLEASE'.

15 ml/½ fl. oz. sugar syrup (2:1 ratio of sugar to water, heated until the sugar dissolves)

3 mint sprigs

60 ml/2 fl. oz. bourbon

Muddle (see page 8) the sugar, one mint sprig and the bourbon in a rocks glass. Add crushed ice and garnish with the remaining mint sprigs. Serve with two straws.

AMERICANO

THE FIRST COCKTAIL TO APPEAR IN THE
BOND BOOKS, THIS REFRESHING BLEND OF
BITTER AND SWEET IS TOPPED WITH SODA
TO MAKE THE IDEAL THIRST-QUENCHER ON
A SUMMER'S DAY.

25 ml/³/₄ fl. oz. Campari

25 ml/³/₄ fl. oz. sweet vermouth

soda water, to top up

an orange slice, to garnish

Build the ingredients over ice in a highball glass, then stir and serve with an orange slice.

CUBA LIBRE

IN *GOLDENEYE* AND *DIE ANOTHER DAY*, BOND VISITS THE TROPICAL ISLAND OF CUBA. MIX YOURSELF A CUBA LIBRE, LIGHT UP A CIGAR (WHY NOT?), THEN SETTLE IN FOR AN EXOTIC NIGHT OF PUNS UNDER PALM TREES, BEAUTIES ON THE BEACH AND WAVES CRASHING CLIMACTICALLY.

15 ml/½ fl. oz. freshly squeezed lime juice, plus the lime shell, to garnish

50 ml/1²/₃ fl. oz. Bacardi Superior rum

150 ml/5 fl. oz. cola

Take a highball and fill it with ice. Squeeze the lime juice in there, then drop the spent lime shell in the glass. Add the rum and cola, stir well and serve. Cuba Libre!

SINGAPORE SLING

THE SINGAPORE SLING WAS INVENTED AT THE FIVE-STAR RAFFLES HOTEL IN SINGAPORE. WHETHER HE'S DRINKING IN THE BAR OR UPSTAIRS 'ENTERTAINING' A GUEST, JAMES BOND IS NO STRANGER TO LAVISH, FIVE-STAR TREATMENT.

35 ml/1¼ fl. oz. Tanqueray gin

15 ml/½ fl. oz. Heering Cherry Liqueur or cherry brandy

1 barspoon Bénédictine D.O.M.

15 ml/½ oz. freshly squeezed lemon juice

2 dashes of Angostura bitters

a splash of soda, to top up

a slice of lemon, to garnish

Build the ingredients into a chilled highball glass filled with cubed ice, give it a quick stir and top with a splash of soda. Garnish with the lemon.

ODDJOB: ONE-OFFS

ODDJOB – AURIC GOLDFINGER'S PERSONAL CHAUFFEUR, BODYGUARD AND GOLF CADDY – IS A PECULIAR LITTLE FELLA, WHO DELIGHTS IN DECAPITATING STONE STATUES WITH HIS RAZOR-EDGED BOWLER HAT. LIKE THIS POPULAR DIMINUTIVE HENCHMAN, THESE COCKTAILS ARE STRONG, STRANGE AND IN A CLASS OF THEIR OWN. AHA!

OLD-FASHIONED

NOT SEEN IN THE FILMS BUT FEATURING IN THE *DIAMONDS ARE FOREVER*, *LIVE AND LET DIE* AND *THUNDERBALL* BOOKS, THE OLD-FASHIONED IS ALMOST ALWAYS TAKEN AS A DOUBLE BY BOND.

1 sugar cube

2 dashes Angostura bitters

50 ml/1²/₃ fl. oz. rye whiskey or bourbon

an orange zest, to garnish

Muddle (see page 8) all the ingredients in a rocks glass, adding ice as you go. Garnish with an orange zest and serve.

BLACK VELVET

IN THE *DIAMONDS ARE FOREVER* NOVEL, BOND
AND MI6'S CHIEF OF STAFF, BILL TANNER,
STOP BY LONDON RESTAURANT SCOTT'S FOR
'DRESSED CRAB AND A PINT OF BLACK
VELVET'. BOND HAS ALSO BEEN KNOWN TO
QUAFF HIS CHAMPAGNE 'NEAT'. BOLLINGER
WAS DUBBED THE 'OFFICIAL' BOND
CHAMPAGNE AFTER BEING SEEN IN 10 OF
THE FILMS.

Guinness

Champagne

Half fill a champagne flute with
Guinness, gently top with
Champagne and serve.

PINK GIN

BOND ORDERS A PINK GIN IN *THE MAN WITH THE GOLDEN GUN* NOVEL, ASKING FOR BEEFEATER AND 'PLENTY OF BITTERS'. DON'T LET THE PRETTY HUE FOOL YOU: THIS TIPPLE IS CERTAINLY TOUGH ENOUGH FOR THE WORLD'S MOST DARING SPY.

50 ml/1²/₃ fl. oz. gin

a dash of Angostura bitters

Rinse a frosted sherry or martini glass with Angostura bitters, add chilled gin and serve.

JAMES BOND

THROUGHOUT THE BOND FILMS, VODKA – THE KEY INGREDIENT IN THIS COCKTAIL – HAS FEATURED WIDELY. IN *DR. NO*, SMIRNOFF WAS THE ENDORSED VODKA BRAND, BUT WAS REPLACED BY STOLICHNAYA IN *A VIEW TO A KILL*. THEN IN *DIE ANOTHER DAY*, FINLANDIA WAS THE VODKA DU JOUR. AHH, PRODUCT PLACEMENT.

25 ml/¾ fl. oz. vodka

1 white sugar cube

2 dashes of Angostura bitters

Champagne

Moisten the sugar cube with Angostura bitters and put into a martini glass. Cover the sugar cube with the vodka and top with champagne.

The James Bond cocktail is depicted on the right of the two drinks shown opposite.

SILVER STREAK

BOND WOULDN'T BE BOND WITHOUT A COOL CAR. MANY OF THESE CLASSICS WERE CLAD IN SILVER, INCLUDING THE ICONIC ASTON MARTIN DB5 AND THE ELEGANT ROLLS ROYCE SILVER CLOUD II. THE LATTER, WHICH FEATURED IN *A VIEW TO A KILL*, WAS ACTUALLY PRODUCER CUBBY BROCCOLI'S CAR.

25 ml/¾ fl. oz. chilled vodka

25 ml/¾ fl. oz. kummel

Pour a generous single measure of chilled vodka into a rocks glass filled with ice. Add a similar amount of kummel, stir gently and serve.

INDEX

PICTURE CREDITS